Trams, Trolleybuses & Recollections
1958 Part 2 June to December

Henry Conn

First published in 2022

British Library Cataloguing in Publication Data

A catalogue record for this book is available from the British Library.

ISBN 978 1 85794 602 4
Silver Link Books
Mortons Media Group Limited
Media Centre
Morton Way
Horncastle
LN9 6JR
Tel/Fax: 01507 529535

email: sohara@mortons.co.uk
Website: www.nostalgiacollection.com

Printed and bound in the Czech Republic

Contents

Acknowledgements

I would like to express my sincere thanks to David and John Clarke for allowing continuing and much appreciated access to their wonderful collection of negatives and slides. All the portraits in this book come from their 1958 collection, and all, bar one, have never been published before.

Introduction

This book is a companion to *Buses, Coaches, Trolleybuses, Trams & Recollections*, No 60 in the series, and *Trams and Trolleybuses 1958 Part 1* No 123 in the series which also covered the year 1958 and were published by Silver Link in 2016 and 2021. This third book concentrates on the trams of Glasgow, Leeds and Sheffield and the trolleybuses of London through the travels of brothers David and John Clarke. In these views taken between 25 June and 6 December, we see a multitude of locations, either no longer existing or changed beyond recognition – quiet roads with little traffic, the period cars and lorries, the fashions, the advertisements of long-lost products, the shops, the buildings and the churches.

Enjoy the nostalgia!

Title page: **SHEFFIELD** This panoramic view of Prince of Wales Road was taken on 10 April 1958, and heading for Darnall is Roberts car No 511. The tramway reservation still remains although it has long since grassed over. *David Clarke*

Left: **GLASGOW** This is Standard hex-dash car No 77 at Parliamentary Road, a major street in the Townhead area of the city. However, a combination of slum clearance and the subsequent construction of the Townhead B housing estate in the 1960s, and later the construction of Buchanan Street Bus Station in the late 1970s, saw a complete rearrangement of the roads in the area. *David Clarke*

Below left: **GLASGOW** The last of the seven views from 25 June was taken at 3.44 in the afternoon. This is Standard hex-dash car 165 on Parliamentary Road near the junction with North Hanover Street. Route 32 was replaced on 15 November 1958 with bus service 55 and extra cars on route 55. *David Clarke*

Below: **GLASGOW** It is now 26 June, the date of the next 11 pictures. The first view was taken at 10.54am and shows Cunarder No 1337 on Keppochhill Road at its junction with Crichton Street. *David Clarke*

Above: **GLASGOW** At Hawthorn Street near its junction with Blackthorn Street is Standard hex-dash car No 172. Standard round-dash No 895 can just be glimpsed under the bridge. *David Clarke*

Above right: **GLASGOW** This is Possilpark depot, which had a capacity for more than 130 trams; due to tight curves, only Standard cars were allocated. Tramcar operations ceased on 6 June 1959 and all cars were transferred to Partick and Maryhill the following day. Outside Possilpark depot at 11.38am is Standard hex-dash car No 123. *David Clarke*

Right: **GLASGOW** At Bilsland Drive railway bridge is Cunarder No 1388, new in 1951. Red Hackle, a blend produced by Hepburn & Ross of Glasgow, was named after the red feather that adorns the hats of the Black Watch. Established in 1920, the company had a policy of hiring ex-military personnel, and the blended whisky became very popular in military bases during the Second World War. It is sadly no longer in production, but at auction today £15 can buy you a bottle. *David Clarke*

GLASGOW Working route 23 to Maryhill at Queens Cross is Coronation No 1204, new in 1938. There's a policeman in the middle of the crowd of people trying to get on to the tram – a hint of trouble maybe, or just off duty. *David Clarke*

Left: **GLASGOW** Opened on 19 December 1927 by Blythswood Picture House Ltd, the Blythswood cinema originally had seating for 1,100; it closed 10 August 1972, and was then used for bingo before being demolished in 1980 to make way for flats. Passing the Blythswood on Maryhill Road is ex-Liverpool No 1038; the Liverpool cars were wider than the Glasgow vehicles and had limited route availability. *David Clarke*

Right: **GLASGOW** On Maryhill Road at St Georges Cross are ex-Liverpool Nos 1030 and 1035. In 1953 and 1954, with the impending closure of Liverpool's tram system in 1957, 46 of that city's relatively modern streamlined bogie trams were purchased by Glasgow Corporation to replace some of the ageing Standard cars. The acquired cars had been built in 1936-37 and were contemporaries of Glasgow's own Coronation trams, with which they were inevitably compared. At 36 feet they were 2 feet longer than the Coronations; accordingly they were normally confined to only two routes, 15 and 29, with relatively few sharp curves. They were not wholly successful in Glasgow as their original construction had not been as robust as that of the Coronations, and with the running-down of the Liverpool system they had been allowed to deteriorate into a poor condition. They therefore had a relatively short time in service in Glasgow; the last was withdrawn in July 1960, more than two years before the final closure of the tramway system. *David Clarke*

GLASGOW This is the junction of New City Road and Cambridge Street, and working route 30 is Standard hex-dash car No 183. On the left is an unidentified ex-Liverpool car working route 29. *David Clarke*

Above: **GLASGOW** This is Cunarder No 1351 in Sauchiehall Street at its junction with Hope Street. The Rover 75 was first registered in Gloucester. *David Clarke*

Above right: **GLASGOW** On Hope Street with West George Street to the left is ex-Liverpool No 1041 on route 29 to Maryhill. The 29 to and from Milngavie and Maryhill to Tollcross and Broomhouse had several sharp curves in the city centre such as Argyle Street/Hope Street, Hope Street/Cowcaddens, and Cowcaddens/New City Road, yet the Liverpool cars managed them with little difficulty. *David Clarke*

Right: **GLASGOW** This view of the St Vincent Street upper crossover at 1.55 in the afternoon is the last view taken on 26 June. The tram is Standard hex-dash No 95. *David Clarke*

Above: **GLASGOW** The following eight pictures were taken on 27 June, and in Saracen Street at 9.20 in the morning, working route 33, the Springburn Circle, is Standard hex-dash car No 41. The Springburn Circle would be withdrawn without replacement on 2 May 1959. The Cowlairs Co-operative Society building on the left was located at 175 to 189 Saracen Street, and the building is still there. *David Clarke*

Above right: **GLASGOW** At the junction of Sauchiehall Street and Cambridge Street 15 minutes later at 9.35 is Cunarder No 1336, new in 1950. Behind it is Coronation No 1198, new in 1938. The cars in view are an Austin A30, a Jaguar Mark VIII and a Hillman Husky three-door estate, which accelerated from 0 to 50mph in just over 24 seconds, while the Jaguar did 0 to 60mph in just over 13 seconds – mind you, at 17 miles per gallon! *John Clarke*

Right: **GLASGOW** At 9.45 we see a very busy scene in Sauchiehall Street at its junction with Hope Street. Standard hex dash car No 231 is working route 22 to Lambhill. *John Clarke*

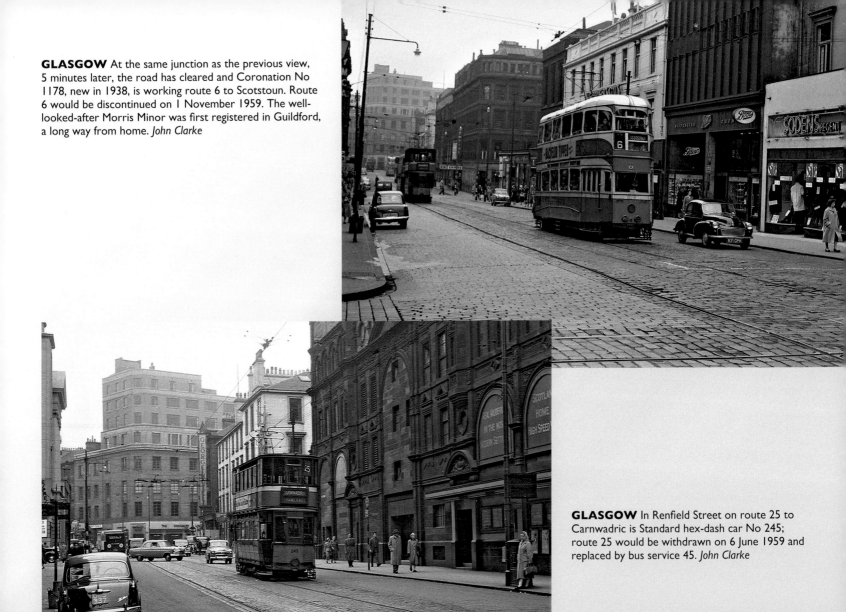

GLASGOW At the same junction as the previous view, 5 minutes later, the road has cleared and Coronation No 1178, new in 1938, is working route 6 to Scotstoun. Route 6 would be discontinued on 1 November 1959. The well-looked-after Morris Minor was first registered in Guildford, a long way from home. *John Clarke*

GLASGOW In Renfield Street on route 25 to Carnwadric is Standard hex-dash car No 245; route 25 would be withdrawn on 6 June 1959 and replaced by bus service 45. *John Clarke*

Above: **GLASGOW** This is North Fredrick Street at 10.00am, and this is Cunarder No 1338. The car in pursuit is a Rover 75, this one having the updated body that was announced on 7 October 1954 and had a bigger boot, a big back window and flashing indicators. *John Clarke*

Above right: **GLASGOW** Coronation No 1252 has just exited Dennistoun depot at 4.50 in the afternoon on a special depot working by way of Duke Street, Bluevale Street crossover, reverse, then Cumbernauld Road to Aitken Street crossover, reverse, then to Alexandra Parade to begin service. John Wallace & Sons produced agricultural implements. *John Clarke*

Right: **GLASGOW** The last view in this sequence, taken at 5.38 in the evening, shows the unique No 1089, built in 1926 in Yoker, on an increasingly miserable and wet 27 June; it will be working on a shipyard special, either Clydebank to Duntocher or Partick to Dalmuir. *John Clarke*

LEEDS The next six views were taken on 7 July, and on Halton Hill is Feltham No 535. By late 1956 Leeds had nearly 80 Felthams still in service, and by the end of the tram service in 1959 there were more Feltham trams in the Leeds fleet than any other single type, though a Feltham was not the very last tram to run in the city. *David Clarke*

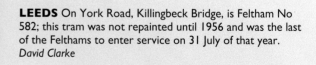

LEEDS On York Road, Killingbeck Bridge, is Feltham No 582; this tram was not repainted until 1956 and was the last of the Felthams to enter service on 31 July of that year. *David Clarke*

LEEDS On the long reserved track section on the York Road near Selby Road Junction, this is Feltham No 574. This was another of the Felthams that was not repainted until 1955, having been with Leeds since 1952. *David Clarke*

LEEDS At the junction of York Road and Selby Road at 12.19pm is Feltham No 535. The Feltham trams were not used on routes 2 and 3 to Moortown and Roundhay until September 1957, when the closure of route 2 meant that they would not need to take a very sharp curve at Moortown Corner. *David Clarke*

Above: **LEEDS** Feltham No 515 is on York Road with Gipton Approach on the right. No 515 was new to Metropolitan Electric Tramways as No 349 in 1931 and passed to London Passenger Transport Board as No 2093 in July 1933. Acquired by Leeds, it was repainted in Leeds livery on 7 January 1951, entering service on 26 January 1951. It had a second repaint on 11 April 1954 and was withdrawn on 30 April 1959. *David Clarke*

Above right: **LEEDS** The last view taken by David Clarke that day was in Middleton Woods at 2.21 in the afternoon, and shows Feltham No 589. The last day of trams running through Middleton Woods would be Saturday 28 March 1959. *David Clarke*

Left: **LEEDS** Feltham No 531 is in York Road, I think near Victoria Primary School, at 9.55am. No 531 was built in 1931 and acquired by Leeds in 1951, entering service in April of that year. *David Clarke*

Below: **LONDON** All the trolleybus route 662 views were taken on 22 July. Route 662 worked from Sudbury to Paddington and was in general a relatively quiet route apart from Saturdays if there were football games on at Wembley Stadium. At Warwick Avenue at 11.37am is No 343 (CUL 343). *John Clarke*

Left: **LEEDS** Passing the Shaftesbury cinema at 9.21am on 8 July is Feltham No 506. The Shaftesbury was opened by Sir Charles Wilson MP on Saturday 20 October 1928 with the film *Beau Geste*, together with, on stage, the Black Dyke Band. The cinema was in an Art Deco style with a seating capacity of 1,603, with the good news for couples that a number of the seats were double. Behind the screen was a large stage measuring 25 feet by 26 feet, which was used to hold live concerts, with Cliff Richard appearing there in 1959. Five months after opening, a large ballroom was added to the building. Initially it was owned by Eddie Anderton, a haulage contractor turned cinema proprietor, but in 1939 it was taken over by Associated British Cinemas, which continued to operate it until it was closed on 27 June 1958. Star Cinemas took over and resumed films until 27 October 1962; at around that time the Shaftesbury became a casino, but reopened as a cinema from 19 October 1964, finally closing on 25 June 1975 with *Death Wish* and *Bad Company*. *David Clarke*

Right: **LONDON** This view was taken from Westbourne Terrace, and working a 662 to Sudbury is No 291 (CUL 291) – note that it has 'spats'-type mudguards. The North Thames Gas van is a Morris/Austin LD. These were produced in Birmingham at Adderley Park, which had been part of the Morris empire. The Austin was badged as the 1-ton van LD1, and the 1½-ton LD2 was launched in December 1954 and produced until 1967. *John Clarke*

Below: **LONDON** In Harrow Road at its junction with Chippenham Road at midday is No 558 (DLY 558). This was one of the E1 Class, consisting of 50 vehicles that were originally allocated to Ilford, Walthamstow and West Ham depots. All of Walthamstow's E1s, and a number of West Ham's, later moved to Stonebridge. *John Clarke*

Below right: **LONDON** At Portnall Road at its junction with Harrow Road is No 281 (CUL 281). This trolleybus operated from Stonebridge depot until withdrawal in August 1959. At peak times route 662 operated a 2-to-3-minute headway. *John Clarke*

Left: **LONDON** Negotiating roadworks at Fourth Avenue in Kensal Green is No 558 (DLY 558), another of the E1 Class vehicles that were reallocated to Stonebridge after the mid-1950s service cuts. *John Clarke*

Right: **LONDON** This view was taken in Ladbroke Grove, and No 251 (CUL 251) is working to Paddington and will pick up goodly numbers of passengers, as the 662 had very little assistance from other London Transport routes. *John Clarke*

Above: **LONDON** On Harrow Road passing Kensal Green Cemetery is No 299 (CUL 299); coming into view, and not 2 to 3 minutes behind is No 286 (CUL 286). Kensal Green Cemetery was opened in 1833 and extends to 72 acres, which includes two conservation areas. *John Clarke*

Above right: **LONDON** Nearing Bow Church in east London is No 1622 (FXH 622). The van is a Fordson E83W, built in Dagenham. In January 1959 the 695 route was withdrawn and route 663 was extended to Chadwell Heath. *John Clarke*

Right: **LONDON** Route 661 started at Lea Bridge depot, and travelled through Whipps Cross, Leytonstone, Stratford and Bow to Aldgate. On High Street, Bow, at its junction with Sugar House Lane is No 1643 (FXH 643). *John Clarke*

Above: **LONDON** Working route 663 between Ilford and Aldgate is No 1573 (FXH 573). This view was taken on the High Street in Stratford at its junction with Ward Road. The overtaking cars are a Morris Oxford and a Hillman Minx. *John Clarke*

Above right: **LONDON** Passing Stratford Market station on route 661 to Aldgate is No 1619 (FXH 619). Stratford Market station closed on 6 May 1957 and the buildings seen on the right of this view were boarded up by the mid-1960s. *John Clarke*

Right: **LONDON** At midday on 23 July, heading east to Ilford Broadway, is No 1581 (FXH 581). Route 663 ran a very frequent service but was in competition with bus route 25 and the route was withdrawn in August 1959. *John Clarke*

LONDON At the junction of Romford Road and Woodgrange Road, nearest the camera is No 605 (DLY 605) on route 685 to Crooked Billet. The 685 normally operated between Crooked Billet and Canning Town, but some operated to Victoria Docks and Silvertown Station, and a some as far as North Woolwich, but only a few travelled all the way from Crooked Billet to North Woolwich. On the right, working a 663 service to Ilford Broadway, is No 1616 (FXH 616). *John Clarke*

Above: **LONDON** This view was taken at the junction of Romford Road and Station Road, and approaching the camera on route 695 to Bow Church is No 1622 (FXH 622). Travelling in the opposite direction, the car is a Leeds-registered Vauxhall Cresta. *John Clarke*

Above right: **LONDON** At Ilford Broadway on 23 July, and working a 663 to Aldgate, is No 1573 (FXH 573). As mentioned earlier, the 663 was extended to Chadwell Heath on 7 January 1959; this extension lasted until 14 August 1959, making it one of the shortest-lived on the whole system. *John Clarke*

Right: **LONDON** On Hainault Street working route 691 to Barking Broadway is No 1729 (GLB 729), one of the 8-foot-wide-bodied SA Class intended for service in South Africa but diverted to London Transport. When Ministry of Transport approval was given, they were only allowed to work routes out of Ilford depot, the 691 and 693. *John Clarke*

Right: **LONDON** At Seven Kings station working route 693 is No 1748 (GLB 748). The front axles of the SA Class were 8 feet wide, the back ones 7ft 6in wide, and this resulted in a body overhang, as can be seen in this view. *John Clarke*

Below: **LONDON** On the High Road at Chadwell Heath at its junction with Reynolds Avenue is No 1607 (FXH 607) working route 695. *John Clarke*

Below right: **LONDON** Working route 693, Chadwell Heath and Barking, this is No 1759 (GLB 759). The route and destination aperture of the SAs was completely different from the standard London trolleybus and special blinds were made. *John Clarke*

LONDON This is the last view taken on 23 July. At Chadwell Heath on route 693 is No 1752 (GLB 752). Even though the SAs were among the newer vehicles operated by London Transport, they had all gone to the scrapyard by February 1960, a lot earlier than many older trolleybuses. *John Clarke*

SHEFFIELD With the Wicker Arch in the background, climbing Spital Hill on 16 August is Standard domed-roof No 290. The car on the right nearest the camera is a Vauxhall Cresta, probably new in 1957 as the two-tone colour scheme for the car was not introduced until late 1956. All the Sheffield views that follow were taken on 16 August. *David Clarke*

Above: **SHEFFIELD** Showing the normal large numerals associated with the old lined-out livery, this is Standard No 63 in Burngreave Road at 1 o'clock in the afternoon. *David Clarke*

Above right: **SHEFFIELD** On Firth Park Road just passing the Page Hall Road junction is Standard domed-roof No 269. The car with the sun-visor is a Morris Oxford Series III with two-tone paintwork, again making it new in 1957. Behind the tram is a Volkswagen Type 2 split-screen van, which was produced from March 1950 until 1967. *David Clarke*

Right: **SHEFFIELD** At the junction of Firth Park Road with Firth Park Avenue, with the Park on the left, is Standard domed-roof car No 299. *David Clarke*

Above: **SHEFFIELD** Metropolitan-Vickers Electrical Company Ltd (Metrovicks) built an armament factory on Attercliffe Common in Sheffield in 1921, a 9-acre site for the manufacture of traction motors. In 1923 it was made into a self-contained traction motor factory with its own engineering department for the manufacture of complete locomotives and electric delivery vehicles; the works closed in 1985. Passing the Attercliffe Road factory at 4.05 in the afternoon is Standard No 27. *David Clarke*

Left: **SHEFFIELD** A little later, at 4.23, we see Roberts No 514 at Vulcan Road terminus. Behind are the buildings of Hadfield steelworks; in 1977 Hadfields became part of Tiny Rowlands's Lonrho. The over-capacity of Britain's steel industry forced the closure of the Leeds Road plant in June 1981 and the East Hecla workforce was much reduced. Lonrho finally closed the last part of Hadfields in 1983, and this location has now completely disappeared, replaced by the Meadowhall shopping complex. *David Clarke*

LEEDS By the late 1920s the existing trams operated by both the Metropolitan Electric Tramways and the London United Tramways were increasingly aged. The two operators cooperated in the development of, arguably, one of the most important types of tram ever built in Britain, the Feltham, and the production vehicles had all entered service by the early 1930s. However, the London Passenger Transport Board plans for converting tram routes to trolleybus operation soon saw these modern cars transferred from the north to the south of the River Thames. There the production cars mostly survived until the final conversion programme, and 90 were sold to Leeds; this is Feltham No 514 on York Road on 4 October. *David Clarke*

Above: **LEEDS** At the Balm Road crossover Feltham No 546 picks up passengers at 1.25 in the afternoon for the journey to Belle Isle. The lorry behind the tram is an elderly Albion. *David Clarke*

Right: **LEEDS** An extension of the Middleton and Belle Isle lines met in 1949 to make a circular tram route. When this final extension was up and running, all trams travelling from town to what had been the Belle Isle terminus bore the route title 27 BELLE ISLE, while those that carried on round, then down into town through Middleton Woods bore the legend 26 MIDDLETON CIRCULAR. Feltham No 526 is at Belle Isle Circus at 1.45pm, working route 26. *David Clarke*

Above: **LEEDS** Fifteen minutes later this is Feltham No 512 at Belle Isle; this tram would be in service on the last day of tram operations in Leeds, on a foggy and damp Saturday 7 November 1959. *David Clarke*

Above right: **LEEDS** This is Feltham 568 on the Middleton Ring Road at its junction with Sharp Lane. No 568 did not enter service with Leeds until late 1955 and was sold for scrap to George Cohen in August 1959. *David Clarke*

Right: **LEEDS** Of the 104 Horsfields built, only four were produced in-house, the other 100 being contracted to Brush. The reason for this was probably that the Kirkstall Road Woks was fully occupied with repairs and routine overhauls. Also, producing 100 cars in ten months was far quicker than Kirkstall Road could manage, and this is probably another reason for contracting out their construction. The Brush-built cars were delivered in two halves, which were joined together at Kirkstall Road. A modern touch, for the 1930s, was the fitting of driving mirrors; these were also being retro-fitted to older cars at this time. The Horsfields also had windscreen wipers, manually operated, and air gauges. At Middleton layby are Horsfields Nos 171 and 185. *David Clarke*

Right: **LEEDS** The last view taken on 4 October, at 2.30 in the afternoon, shows Horsfield No 179 passing the Middleton Arms. The Middleton Arms opened as a hotel in 1925 and boasted a ballroom that was painted with murals. It also had its own private double tennis courts and sunken garden. Unfortunately the pub was set ablaze on 3 December 2011, and an Aldi store stands in its place. *David Clarke*

Below: **LEEDS** No 515 has just passed under Halton Dial railway bridge at 10.30am on 25 October. Appleyard of Leeds had large premises at the intersections of North Street, Roundhay Road, Chapeltown Road, Sheepscar Street North, and Sheepscar Street South. *David Clarke*

Below right: **LONDON** Route 666 commenced on 5 July 1936, operating between Hammersmith and Edgware, and for most of its operation was a peak-hour service that only became daily in January 1959. This view of No 302 (CUL 302) was taken at Atwood Road, Hammersmith, on 23 October at 2.30 in the afternoon. *John Clarke*

LONDON Hammersmith was also the starting point for route 660, which had commenced on 5 April 1936 between Hammersmith and Acton Market Place. The service was withdrawn in July of that year but reintroduced on 2 August 1936, operating from Hammersmith to North Finchley. This view was taken on 23 October at the Seven Stars Junction, and heading for Hammersmith is No 561 (DLY 561). *John Clarke*

LONDON At the Angel at 10.30am on 1 November is No 1411 (FXH 411) working route 615 to Moorgate. Moorgate was an important terminus serving six routes, the 609, 611, 615, 639, 641 and 683. Route 615 was between Moorgate and Parliament Hill Fields, passing through King's Cross and Islington. *John Clarke*

Above: **LONDON** At Finsbury Square north side, working route 611 between Moorgate and Highgate Village, is No 1356 (EXV 356). *John Clarke*

Above right: **LONDON** On the east side of Finsbury Square, heading to Parliament Hill Fields on route 615, is No 1415 (FXH 415). Overtaking on route 609 from Moorgate to Barnet is No 964 (ELB 964); the other three trolleybuses in this view were noted as Nos 762, 1038 and 1045. *John Clarke*

Right: **LONDON** On New North Road at its junction with Bookham Road in Hoxton is No 1049 (EXV 49), working route 611 from Highgate Village to Moorgate. Travelling in the opposite direction is a rather elderly Standard Vanguard Phase 1, which was built between 1947 and 1953. *John Clarke*

Right: **LONDON** On Balls Pond Road is No 1333 (EXV 333), working from Bloomsbury to Woodford. Three routes terminated at Bloomsbury, the 555, 581 and 665; route 581's final day of operation was 14 April 1959. *John Clarke*

Left: **LONDON** Also in Balls Pond Road, heading in the opposite direction while working route 683 to Moorgate, is No 1202, (EXV 202). By the time this view was taken, the 683 was peak hours only. *John Clarke*

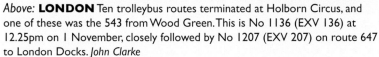

Above: **LONDON** Ten trolleybus routes terminated at Holborn Circus, and one of these was the 543 from Wood Green. This is No 1136 (EXV 136) at 12.25pm on 1 November, closely followed by No 1207 (EXV 207) on route 647 to London Docks. *John Clarke*

Above right: **LONDON** On Stamford Hill at its junction with Manor Road on route 683 to Moorgate is No 1137 (EXV 137). There seems to be a problem with the elderly Austin Seven, as indicated by the gentleman whose feet are not touching the ground! *John Clarke*

Right: **LONDON** Working route 649, Waltham Cross to Liverpool Street, on Stamford Hill at its junction with Portland Avenue is No 1686 (GGP 686). The trolleybus terminus for the 649 was near Liverpool Street station, with a turn at Bishopsgate. *John Clarke*

Above: **LONDON** At the Stamford Hill terminus of route 647 is No 1112 (EXV 112), and noted behind it is No 1326 (EXV 326), which would be the last trolleybus to enter Stamford Hill depot on 19 July 1961 at the cessation of operations. *John Clarke*

Above right: **LONDON** At 2.00pm on 1 November on the north side of Finsbury Square working a 683 to Stamford Hill is No 1137 (EXV 137). I think the sports car in the background is an early-1950s Morgan Plus 4. *John Clarke*

Right: **LONDON** On Pentonville Road working route 639 from Moorgate to Hampstead Heath is No 1373 (EXV 373). *John Clarke*

Right: **LONDON** The 613 Holborn Circus to Hampstead Heath route was never a great money-spinner, but the route did pass the important railway stations of King's Cross and St Pancras. At King's Cross at 2.50pm is No 1320 (EXV 320). *John Clarke*

Below: **LONDON** The Hampstead Heath and Parliament Hill Fields routes were in general only busy in the summer months. In a very quiet Pancras Road between St Pancras (left) and the Great Northern Hotel at King's Cross (right) at 2.55pm is No 753 (DLY 753), on route 615 to Moorgate from Parliament Hill Fields. *John Clarke*

Below right: **LONDON** At Royal College Street on a 615 service to Moorgate is No 1415 (FXH 415). 1 November was a Saturday, and the lack of both people and traffic is quite noticeable. Just over three weeks after this picture was taken the Austin FX4 London taxi went on sale. *John Clarke*

Right: **LONDON** The last view taken on 1
November was at Mornington Crescent station.
Route 653 was a circuitous journey between
Tottenham Court Road and Aldgate via Mile End,
Bethnal Green, Hackney, Stamford Hill, Manor House
and Holloway. Heading to Aldgate is No 1004 (EXV
4). *John Clarke*

Below: **LONDON** At East Acton Lane, Acton, on
5 November is No 1558 (FXH 558) on route 660
from North Finchley to Hammersmith. *John Clarke*

Below right: **LONDON** No 699 (DLY 699) was
one of a large number of F1 Class trolleybuses based
at Hanwell depot, which spent most of their working
service journeying up and down Uxbridge Road
between Shepherds Bush and Uxbridge. A number of
607s only went as far as Hayes End Road, as No 699
indicates in this view. *John Clarke*

LONDON The 666 was always a busy route, although in this view of No 1557 (FXH 557), taken at 2.28pm on Wednesday 5 November, the upper deck appears to be empty and the lower sparsely populated. The location is Market Place, Acton. *John Clarke*

Below right: **LONDON** The background of this view at North Acton is dominated by the Napier factory, which manufactured vehicles and engines. In 1946 Napier won a contract to design and build a diesel engine for the Royal Navy, and the result was the 'Deltic'. Development and production of 'Deltic' engines saw them fitted to British Rail's Type 5 (later Class 55) 'Deltic' locomotives to huge effect. Napier was taken over by Rolls-Royce in 1962. At the west end of North Acton station on route 660 to North Finchley is No 1601 (FXH 601). *John Clarke*

LONDON The main vehicles to be allocated to route 666 from its inception until August 1959 were the C Class; at that time they were replaced by newer vehicles that had been operating from the East End. Representing the C Class on route 666 at King Street, Hammersmith, is No 334 (CUL 334). *John Clarke*

LONDON At the east end of North Acton station, working route **666** to Hammersmith, is No 300 (CUL 300). In the background is the Elizabeth Arden perfume factory. *John Clarke*

LONDON The last view taken on 5 November is from Midland Terrace at its junction with Victoria Road, North Acton; working route 660 to North Finchley is No 1652 (FXH 652). The lonely overtaking car is a Hillman Minx. *John Clarke*

LONDON Route 664 began operations between Paddington and Edgware on 23 August 1936. On Cricklewood Broadway on 29 November working a 664 service to Paddington is No 373 (CUL 373). *John Clarke*

LONDON Route 645 started operation between North Finchley and Edgware on 2 August 1936 and was extended to Canons Park and Barnet on 1 June 1938. This is No 367 (CUL 367) turning on St Gabriel's Church loop, Cricklewood, on 29 November. *John Clarke*

LONDON Route 664 became a peak-hour and weekend service only in May 1956 and was last operated on 6 January 1959. This view of No 1599 (FXH 599) was taken at Willesden Green station at 11.25am on 29 November. No 664 has a little over seven weeks left in operation. *John Clarke*

LONDON The man with the handcart will be waiting for quite a time before traffic clears so that he can cross the road. Passing Paddington Town Hall on route 664 to Edgware on 6 December is 558, (DLY 558). Paddington Town Hall dated from 1853 and following its closure in 1965 was demolished to make way for Westway.
John Clarke

LONDON At Edgware at 1 o'clock in the afternoon on 6 December is No 338 (CUL 338). The driver is reading his paper and there is not a passenger in sight.
John Clarke

1958 Happenings (4)

continued from Part 1

October *(continued)*
Blue Peter is first broadcast
Life Peerages Act entitles women to sit in
House of Lords
Boris Pasternak wins Nobel Prize for
Literature
First transatlantic flight of a Pan-Am
Boeing 707
Pope John XXIII appointed Pope following
death of Pius XII

November
New UNESCO building is inaugurated in
Paris
Bossa nova dance introduced in Rio de
Janeiro
French Sudan, Chad, Republic of the
Congo and Gabon become
autonomous republics within French
colonial empire

December
Subscriber Trunk Dialling (STD)
inaugurated in UK
Preston Bypass, Britain's first stretch of
motorway, is opened
US launches SCORE, world's first
communications satellite
Charles de Gaulle elected President of
France
Rebel troops under Che Guevara invade
Santa Clara, Cuba, and President
Batista resigns two days later

LONDON This is Colindale depot, and noted at 1.24 in the afternoon are, from left to right, Nos 376, 309 and 329 (CUL 376, CUL 309 and CUL 329). After being withdrawn, most London trolleybuses ended up at the scrapyard of Cohen's, at the back of this depot; the C Class trolleybuses in this view did not have far to go. *John Clarke*